I W
Your Case

by Lucy Floyd
illustrations by Jenny Williams

Harcourt Brace & Company

Orlando   Atlanta   Austin   Boston   San Francisco   Chicago   Dallas   New York   Toronto   London

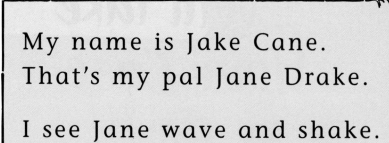

My name is Jake Cane.
That's my pal Jane Drake.

I see Jane wave and shake.
Is Jane in pain? Is Jane
afraid?

2

"A snake!" Jane wails. Jane is afraid of snakes.

"Be brave," I say. "Don't faint. What did the snake look like?"

Snake, plain gray, on Tate's gate.

"It was a plain, gray snake on the Tates' gate. I hate snakes!" says Jane.

"Wait here," I say. I go to Gail Tate's gate. I see wet paint.

TAKE CARE!
WET PAINT.

7

I see wet paint on a blade
of grass. I see a trail of
paint in the shape
of a snake.

8

I see the snake! It's Blake!
Blake is Gail Tate's pet
snake.

9

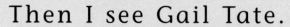

Then I see Gail Tate.
"My snake!" Gail yells.
"My snake got away from his cage!"

"Gail," I say, "here's your snake."
"Jane," I say, "now you're safe."

10

Are YOU afraid? Is YOUR pet snake missing? I will take your case!